FIRST 50 SONGS

YOU SHOULD PLAY ON THE BELLS/GLOCKENSPIEL

ISBN 978-1-5400-7011-1

Visit Hal Leonard Online at
www.halleonard.com

Contact us:
Hal Leonard
7777 West Bluemound Road
Milwaukee, WI 53213
Email: info@halleonard.com

In Europe, contact:
Hal Leonard Europe Limited
42 Wigmore Street
Marylebone, London, W1U 2RN
Email: info@halleonardeurope.com

In Australia, contact:
Hal Leonard Australia Pty. Ltd.
4 Lentara Court
Cheltenham, Victoria, 3192 Australia
Email: info@halleonard.com.au

CONTENTS

ALL OF ME

BELLS

Words and Music by JOHN STEPHENS
and TOBY GAD

Slowly, in 2

5

1.

1st time D.C.
2nd time Fine

2.

D.S. al Fine
(take 1st ending)

ALL YOU NEED IS LOVE

BELLS

Words and Music by JOHN LENNON
and PAUL McCARTNEY

AMAZING GRACE

BELLS

Traditional American Melody

BASIN STREET BLUES

BELLS

Words and Music by
SPENCER WILLIAMS

(small notes optional)

BEST SONG EVER

Bells

Words and Music by EDWARD DREWETT,
WAYNE HECTOR, JULIAN BUNETTA
and JOHN RYAN

CANON IN D

BELLS

JOHANN PACHELBEL

CARNIVAL OF VENICE

BELLS

By JULIUS BENEDICT

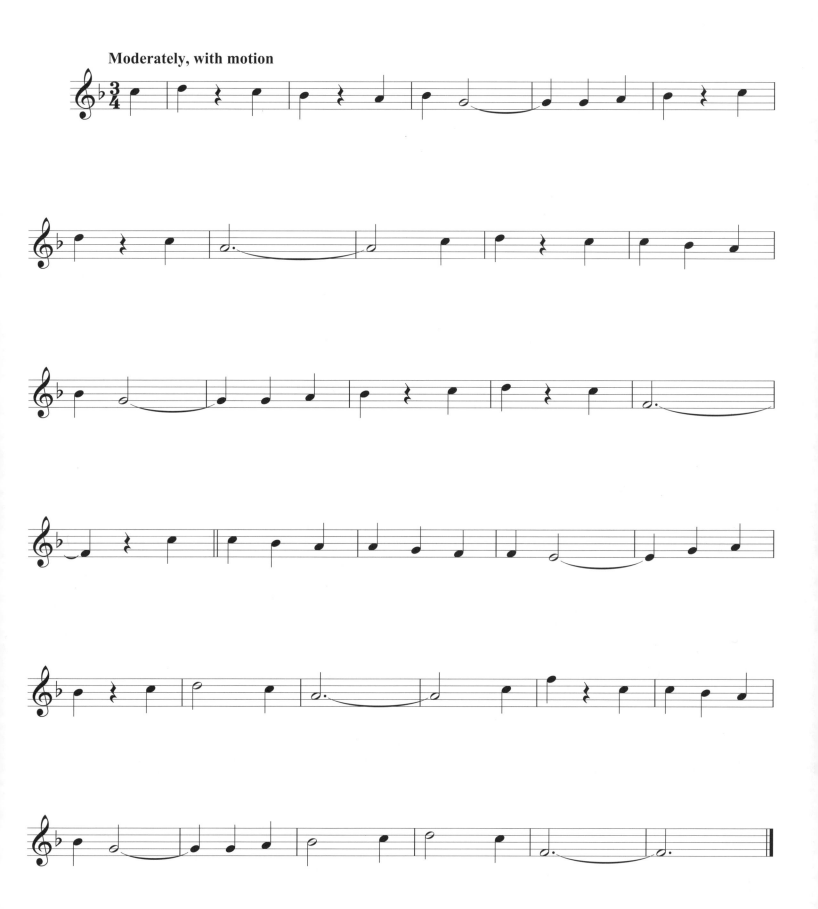

CIRCLE OF LIFE
from THE LION KING

BELLS

Music by ELTON JOHN
Lyrics by TIM RICE

Moderately (with an African beat)

EVERMORE
from BEAUTY AND THE BEAST

BELLS

Music by ALAN MENKEN
Lyrics by TIM RICE

FIGHT SONG

BELLS

Words and Music by RACHEL PLATTEN
and DAVE BASSETT

FLY ME TO THE MOON
(In Other Words)

BELLS

Words and Music by
BART HOWARD

THE FOOL ON THE HILL

BELLS

Words and Music by JOHN LENNON
and PAUL McCARTNEY

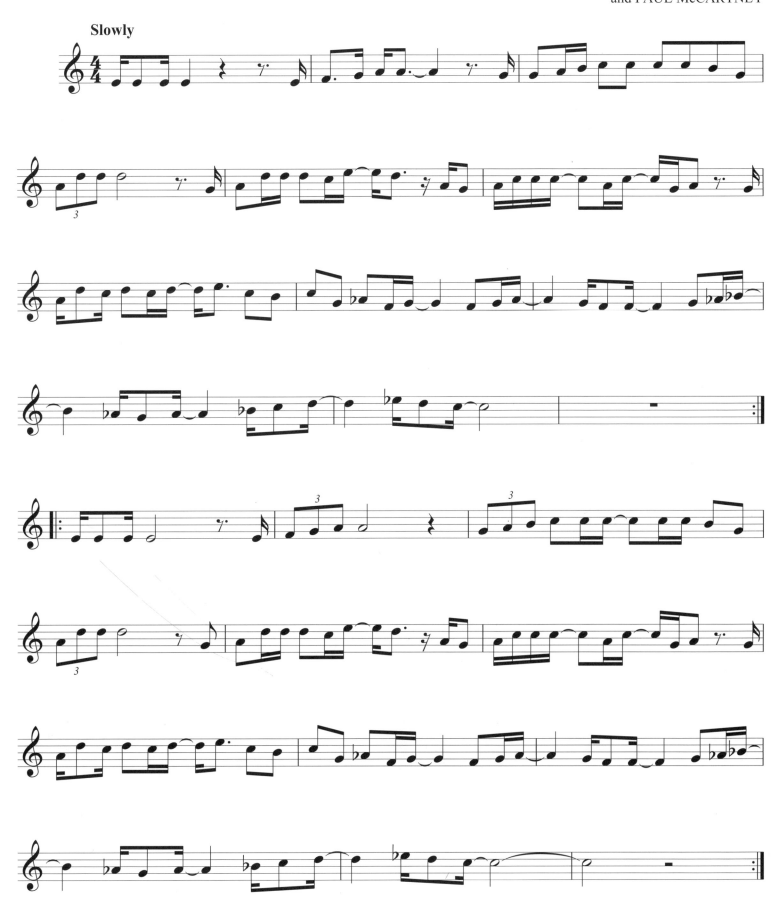

GOD BLESS AMERICA®

BELLS

Words and Music by
IRVING BERLIN

Moderately

THE GODFATHER
(Love Theme)
from the Paramount Picture THE GODFATHER

BELLS

By NINO ROTA

Slowly and expressively

HALLELUJAH

BELLS

Words and Music by
LEONARD COHEN

Moderately slow, in 2

HAPPY
from DESPICABLE ME 2

BELLS

Words and Music by
PHARRELL WILLIAMS

HELLO

BELLS

Words and Music by
LIONEL RICHIE

Slow Ballad

HELLO, DOLLY!

from HELLO, DOLLY!

BELLS

Music and Lyric by
JERRY HERMAN

HOW DEEP IS YOUR LOVE
from the Motion Picture SATURDAY NIGHT FEVER

Bells

Words and Music by BARRY GIBB,
ROBIN GIBB and MAURICE GIBB

THE HUSTLE

BELLS

Words and Music by
VAN McCOY

I WILL ALWAYS LOVE YOU

BELLS

Words and Music by
DOLLY PARTON

Moderately slow

MAS QUE NADA

BELLS

Words and Music by
JORGE BEN

JUST GIVE ME A REASON

Bells

Words and Music by ALECIA MOORE,
JEFF BHASKER and NATE RUESS

CODA

JUST THE WAY YOU ARE

BELLS

Words and Music by BRUNO MARS,
ARI LEVINE, PHILIP LAWRENCE,
KHARI CAIN and KHALIL WALTON

31

LET IT GO
from FROZEN

BELLS

Music and Lyrics by KRISTEN ANDERSON-LOPEZ
and ROBERT LOPEZ

Fine

D.S. al Fine

MY HEART WILL GO ON
(Love Theme from 'Titanic')
from the Paramount and Twentieth Century Fox Motion Picture TITANIC

BELLS

Music by JAMES HORNER
Lyric by WILL JENNINGS

NATURAL

Bells

Words and Music by DAN REYNOLDS,
WAYNE SERMON, BEN McKEE,
DANIEL PLATZMAN, JUSTIN TRANTOR,
MATTIAS LARSSON and ROBIN FREDRICKSSON

NIGHT TRAIN

BELLS

Words by OSCAR WASHINGTON
and LEWIS C. SIMPKINS
Music by JIMMY FORREST

PERFECT

BELLS

Words and Music by
ED SHEERAN

PURE IMAGINATION
from WILLY WONKA AND THE CHOCOLATE FACTORY

Bells

Words and Music by LESLIE BRICUSSE
and ANTHONY NEWLEY

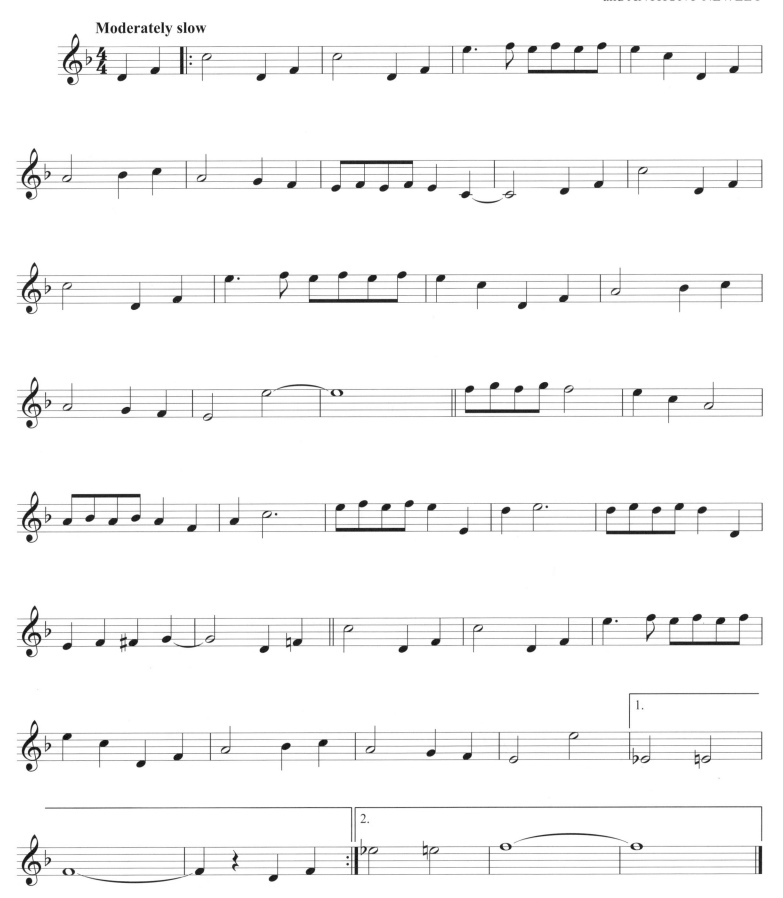

ROAR

BELLS

Words and Music by KATY PERRY,
MAX MARTIN, DR. LUKE,
BONNIE McKEE and HENRY WALTER

Moderately

ROLLING IN THE DEEP

BELLS

Words and Music by ADELE ADKINS
and PAUL EPWORTH

SATIN DOLL

BELLS

By DUKE ELLINGTON

SAY SOMETHING

Bells

Words and Music by IAN AXEL,
CHAD VACCARINO and MIKE CAMPBELL

SCARBOROUGH FAIR/CANTICLE

BELLS

Arrangement and Original Counter Melody by
PAUL SIMON and ARTHUR GARFUNKEL

SHAKE IT OFF

BELLS

Words and Music by TAYLOR SWIFT,
MAX MARTIN and SHELLBACK

SEE YOU AGAIN

from FURIOUS 7

Bells

Words and Music by CAMERON THOMAZ,
CHARLIE PUTH, JUSTIN FRANKS,
ANDREW CEDAR, DANN HUME,
JOSH HARDY and PHOEBE COCKBURN

SHALLOW

from A STAR IS BORN

BELLS

Words and Music by STEFANI GERMANOTTA,
MARK RONSON, ANDREW WYATT
and ANTHONY ROSSOMANDO

SLOOP JOHN B

BELLS

West Indies Folk Song
Arranged by BRIAN WILSON

Moderately

THE SOUND OF SILENCE

BELLS

Words and Music by
PAUL SIMON

STAND BY ME

Words and Music by JERRY LEIBER,
MIKE STOLLER and BEN E. KING

BELLS

THE STAR-SPANGLED BANNER

BELLS

Words by FRANCIS SCOTT KEY
Music by JOHN STAFFORD SMITH

With spirit

STAY WITH ME

BELLS

Words and Music by SAM SMITH,
JAMES NAPIER, WILLIAM EDWARD PHILLIPS,
TOM PETTY and JEFF LYNNE

STOMPIN' AT THE SAVOY

Bells

By BENNY GOODMAN,
EDGAR SAMPSON and CHICK WEBB

Bright Swing

SUMMERTIME

from *PORGY AND BESS*®

BELLS

Music and Lyrics by GEORGE GERSHWIN,
DuBOSE and DOROTHY HEYWARD
and IRA GERSHWIN

TEQUILA

BELLS

By CHUCK RIO

THIS IS ME

from THE GREATEST SHOWMAN

BELLS

Words and Music by BENJ PASEK
and JUSTIN PAUL

Defiantly

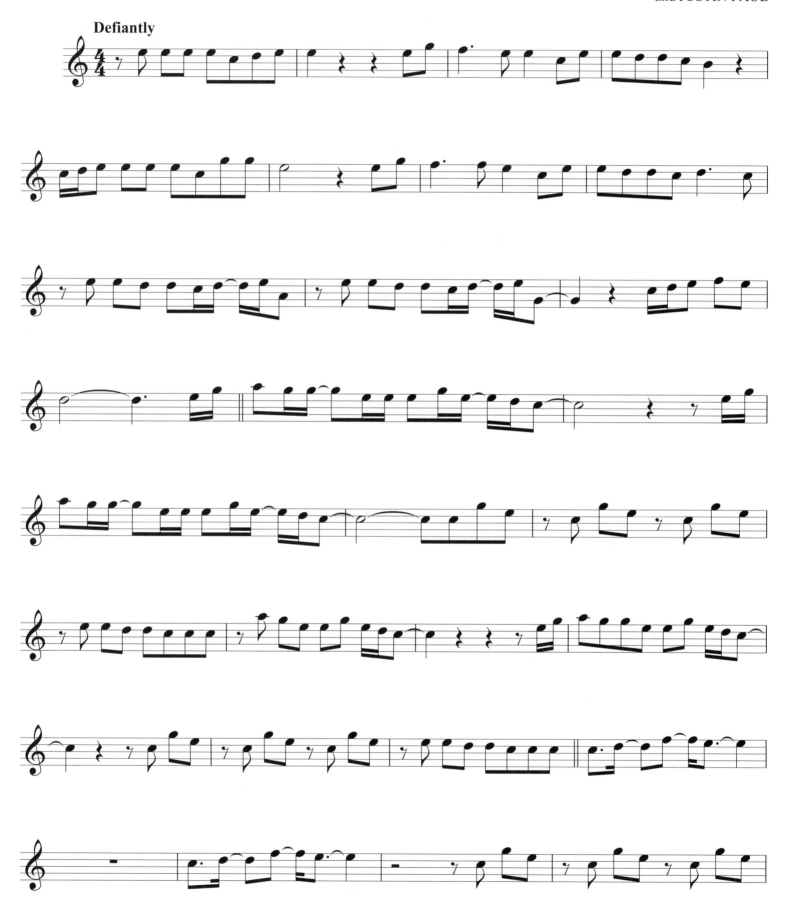

UKRAINIAN BELL CAROL

BELLS

Traditional
Music by MYKOLA LEONTOVYCH

Joyfully

WHAT A WONDERFUL WORLD

Bells

Words and Music by GEORGE DAVID WEISS
and BOB THIELE

UPTOWN FUNK

Bells

Words and Music by MARK RONSON,
BRUNO MARS, PHILIP LAWRENCE, JEFF BHASKER, DEVON GALLASPY,
NICHOLAUS WILLIAMS, LONNIE SIMMONS, RONNIE WILSON,
CHARLES WILSON, RUDOLPH TAYLOR and ROBERT WILSON